I0503662

The Purpose for Work

The Blessing is not burdensome

Andrew Simwanza

Copyright © 2018

Dedications

The work of this book is dedicated to the Holy Spirit. I will not hesitate to mention my wonderful wife, Bupe P. J. Simwanza, my son, Andrew Gracious Simwanza Jr. and my brother, the esteemed Mr. Emmanuel Simwanza. Their immense support is always invaluable

Contact

Andrew Simwanza

Cell Phone (WhataApp): +260 979 235 152

Email: andrewsimwanza@gmail.com

www.andrewsimwanza.wordpress.com

Table of Contents

Introduction

The plan of god is introduced to us in the book of Genesis. His plan was for man to work and find fulfilment. Satan may have thought that he slowed the plan of God, but he did not. In fact, he knew he would not be able to stop it, and so he corrupted what God meant for good.

The LORD is good and what He made for us is good. We have come a long way to be lazy here. We will work, work and work again, because we know the will of the Father toward us.

Enjoy reading.

Chapter 1

The Deceit of Satan

Work is important. There is always a sense of achievement when something is gained as a result of work put in. Take money, for instance, those who work for it tend to spend it more responsibly than the ones who may have ill-gotten it. But there is a certain doctrine which had crept into the Church, unknowingly, encouraging men and women to be lazy and always accept free things.

There are men and women, especially of the Pentecostal movements, who have taught that Adam was free from work; they teach that there was no work in the Garden of Eden.

The most basic definition of work is, "to get something done." If we are to use this definition, then there would be no justification for entertaining the idea that Adam was merely idle and lived work-free. There is a belief that Adam only *laboured* after Sin crept into all creation. Many purport that when the ground was cursed, God caused it to produce thorns and thistles (Genesis 3:17-19); they say that this was what caused the man start sweating for his worth.

Apart from the definition we gave earlier, there could be another reason we should consider that maybe, just maybe, Adam was created to work. The word of God tells us many things about work after the Sin, but it also tells us something about the man's life before he ate the fruit of the tree of the knowledge of good and evil.

If we are to study the scriptures objectively, we will understand that the Father created Adam to work. I do not want to get into a heated debate on why we were created, here. All I need the reader to understand is that there could not have been any reason for the creation excluding work. The Bible shows that the time Adam was created, everything else had already been put in place by God. The man was placed in that Garden to tend to everything and anything in it.

Genesis 2:5, *And every plant of the field before it was in the earth, and every herb of the field before it grew: for the LORD God had not caused it to rain upon the earth, and there was not a man to till the ground.*

The word tells us that the herbs of the field had not grown yet because there was no rain- God had not caused it to rain upon the earth. The other reason is because there was no man to till the ground. God had not created Adam. This means that one of the reasons God put man on the earth was for him to till the ground.

That word, *till,* literally translates, to *cultivate.* The man had not yet been created, and God already had work intentions for him. Do you notice that God could not create the man without wetting the ground?

> **Genesis 2:6-7,** *But there went up a mist from the earth, and watered the whole face of the ground. And the LORD God formed man of the dust of the ground, and breathed into his nostrils the breath of life; and man became a living soul.*

The LORD God formed man of the dust of the ground, but that was after a mist went up from the earth and watered the whole face of the ground; He breathed in him and man became a living soul. So even the Father needed the rains in order to work the ground. The man was created to cultivate the ground in order to produce crop.

Genesis 8:22, While the earth remaineth, seedtime and harvest, and cold and heat, and summer and winter, and day and night shall not cease.

The covenant God had made meant that the seasons He created in the beginning would remain. In other words, God thought about how He changed the seasons, day and night, seed time and harvest in order to punish man-kind. But in this case, after Noah's burnt offering, He made a covenant with him. This means that the laws which governed time and seasons would not change anymore. He is saying He will no longer curse the ground for the sake of man.

Notice that the ground was not cursed before Adam sinned, and yet he still had to abide by the standards and laws set in place by God; the seasons and times existed.

The man was supposed to work by tilling the ground. Without focussing on what happened after the man sinned, we already know that man was created a working man. He needed to work in order to complete the purpose of God for him in the Garden and in the earth. The LORD had instructed the man to keep the Garden. In essence, the caretaker; the man was to have dominion over every living creature in the earth. He said to them, "Be fruitful, and multiply, and replenish the earth, and subdue it: and have dominion over the fish of the sea, and over the fowl of the air, and over every living thing that moves upon the earth; I have given you every herb bearing seed, which *is* upon the face of all the earth, and every tree, in the which *is* the fruit of a tree yielding seed; to you it shall be for meat. And to every beast of the earth, and to every fowl of the air, and to everything that creeps upon the earth, wherein *there is* life, *I have given* every green herb for meat." (Genesis 1:28-30). All this required work in order to be accomplished. Adam was not only supposed to sit and wait for all things to bring themselves under the headship of man; he was supposed to exercise authority in order for those blessings and commands to fall in place.

To work involves a lot of man, as a matter of fact, it involves all of man. Working entails physical, mental, emotional and spiritual exertion. The way a person exerts themselves matters. For instance, Adam was as much a physical being as he was spiritual, intellectual or emotional. Many of the strides he achieved in the Garden required that he exerted himself on those levels in order to get things done. Remember that he needed to name the animals (intellectual), commune with God (Spiritual), till the ground (Physical) and he wasn't ashamed of his nakedness (emotional).

One day, the bible says, God brought all the living creatures to the man to see what he would name them; the names he gave them were their names. This was work. Adam had to think of a name for all the creatures which the LORD presented to him. I can imagine the amount of intellectual effort that took. I can't help but wonder how long it took for him to give names to everything. I also know that Adam was a super man in that he was free from sin and his mind, unpolluted; I believe he went through the process with absolute genius.

All this tells us that the man was always created to do some work. Man was supposed to get things done. Besides, God would not have created the woman if he thought the man did not need help. The woman was placed into the Garden to be a helper; the man was given certain tasks to complete in the Garden and the woman was a suitable help to this work.

We should also consider that if we were created in the image of God, which we were, we are to function as God. The LORD created the man to look and operate just as the Father did; this was the Father's intention. The Father has been working from the beginning.

Genesis 2:2, And on the seventh day God ended his work which he had made; and he rested on the seventh day from all his work which he had made.

One would think that the almighty God has not worked a single day. Well, the Bible tells us differently. We know that God worked from the beginning. There are people who say that the day they discovered what they loved to do they have never worked since. This statement would prove deceitful in light of the scriptures.

The first thing we see God doing in the bible is work. He works by restoring and bringing order and sanity to the world. Even before the Father actually speaks any words, the Holy Spirit was busy hovering above the waters (Genesis 1:2). The Father worked from the first day to the sixth, and He rested on the seventh.

But the enemy has perverted this truth to the utter destruction of many of the people of God. He has blinded the eyes of many Spirit-filled Christians and fed them the lie that work is for the fallen man. This idea goes against everything God planned for the man. Satan has corrupted the thing God had made to bring fulfilment to the man and made it evil.

Many Christians use Genesis 3:19 as basis for this lie. This is what it says:

In the sweat of thy face shalt thou eat bread, till thou return unto the ground; for out of it wast thou taken: for dust thou art, and unto dust shalt thou return.

It is disheartening seeing Children of God wallowing in poverty and self-pity because they have not learnt to work with what they have to better their lives. Now, this is different from the suffering caused by corruption or by men with ill-intentions toward their neighbour. I am talking about people who are only victims of the lie that man was not created to work. Such people believe that working came as a result of the Sin of Adam and Eve, and that the Christian, being free from that *nature,* should expect everything to *work together for the good.* Nothing works until you work it.

The people who have succumbed to such deceit are usually frustrated. There is nothing more frustrating than failing to realize one's dreams. God planned for man to work towards realizing his purpose which God had properly placed in his heart. The only thing which caused Adam to work and not merely loaf in the Garden was the fact that he had a mission; the man had to accomplish the work God gave him in order to find fulfilment. A life without fulfilment would be a very infuriating one.

See what Lamech said about Noah:

Genesis 5:29, *And he called his name Noah, saying, This same shall comfort us concerning our work and toil of our hands, because of the ground which the LORD hath cursed.*

As if Lamech was there when Adam and Eve lived the Sin-less life, he makes a very serious statement concerning the Curse. Adam and Eve lived a life free from toil in the Garden of Eden. Lamech called his son Noah because he hoped that he would comfort them concerning their work and toil of their hands, because of the ground which the LORD had cursed.

Isn't it amazing that Lamech felt the need for comfort concerning not only the toil, but also the work? You would think he enjoyed the work he was left by his father, but to him, he saw the sorrow part of it more than its goodness. There are still many men today, who feel that the toil they are experiencing far outweighs their work. In other words, Lamech felt that he was putting in more than what he was getting; and he hoped that Noah would comfort him and his family.

Genesis 3:23, *Therefore the LORD God sent him forth from the garden of Eden, to till the ground from whence he was taken.*

When the LORD sent the first couple out of the Garden, He actually sent them somewhere. He did not just send them out into the darkness without purpose. God still maintained a certain level of purpose and vision for the man. The purpose had not changed much, the man still needed to work, but the environment had changed. Adam and his family were no longer in the Garden; this time they had to work from outside the Garden.

That is important because the blessing of Eden was not with them. They had to sweat and work in sorrow for them to get anything done.

The amount of toil they needed to put in was far greater than how it was in Eden. This time, for the first time, Adam and Eve felt the sweat excreting from the pores of their skins- they felt how hard physical exertion was over reliance on spiritual capabilities. Adam still had purpose, he just needed to work extra hard in order to realize it.

Did you know that there are people who think that the woman's labour during child-birth is also a result of the Sin? There are those who teach that the labour associated with the woman's work of giving birth is a result of the fall of man by reason of the Sin. This is a very misguided notion as God did intend for the woman to labour in child-bearing from the beginning, but in a normal way.

Ideally, work in the Garden was easy and productive, but when the man and woman were sent out of Eden, it became more difficult to get anything done. In-fact, it became almost impossible without the application of more strenuous effort. Work became more laborious and sorrowful. The same token applied to child-birth.

Genesis 3:16, *Unto the woman he said, I will greatly multiply thy sorrow and thy conception; in sorrow thou shalt bring forth children; and thy desire shall be to thy husband, and he shall rule over thee.*

The context in the above passage suggests that there was already labour involved in childbearing, and after the Sin, the sorrow was multiplied, increased; there cannot be any increase without the existence of that being increased. Even though God had plans for the woman to give birth even before the Sin, it would not have been without the grief and the pangs that come with it. The Sin just made all this sorrow multiply and almost unbearable.

Indeed, the complications of childbirth were not in the plan of God. The five common labour complications include:

1. *Umbilical cord Issues:* This means that the umbilical cord is looped around the baby's neck or otherwise entangled, possibly causing compression.
2. *Perineal lacerations:* A tear in the perineum (the general region between the anus and the genital organs).
3. *Abnormal foetal heart rate or rhythm:* The foetal heart rate goes outside the "normal" range of 110 to 160 beats per minute or the rhythm is unusual.
4. *Amniotic cavity issues:* Too much or too little amniotic fluid or rupturing of the membranes that hold the amniotic fluid

(also known as, your "water breaks") at or beyond 37 weeks

5. *Failure to progress:* Here, labour stalls. This is the most common reason for a Caesarean section (C-Section).

The above conditions and many others may lead to foetal death. But these were not in the plan of God; they are the result of the fallen woman's body as a result of the Sin. The worst thing that could happen to a person would be to give in to the lie that these negative outcomes of the Sin were in the plan of God. These were not in the plan and are still not the work of God. I will end this chapter by pasting a story I wrote and was posted to encouragingdads.com, I hope it blesses you:

Miscarriage, why am I hurting?

A father's tale

I know that there are books and websites out there dedicated to Miscarriage and how to deal with its post-traumatic stresses. This is not one of those. This article does not answer the how and why of the miscarriage. I know that all those resources are available everywhere on the internet. This is only an attempt to answer this question, *"Why am I hurting?"*

But before I go any further, allow me to tell you my story. My wife and I married young. We were so in love that the moment we got married, we wanted a baby right away. After a month in marriage, we discovered she was pregnant with child. I was excited, and so was she. We straight away started preparing for this bundle of joy who was slowly forming inside of her. To us, it felt like this baby was really taking its time in there. The ultrasound revealed that we were going to have a baby boy.

My wife had started going for antenatal visits with the clinic and all seemed normal. One night she felt something moving in her belly. She had felt movement before, but she told me this one was different. I asked her if it was painful, but she wasn't in any pain.

The next morning, I went for work and my wife went to the clinic to be checked. I was in a meeting when she called my phone, the caller ID showed that it was she who was calling. I put the phone on silent intending to call her as soon as the meeting ended. Then she called again. I rushed outside to pick the call and she just went straight to the point, "they said the baby has no heartbeat." "What?" I replied. I asked her how they arrived to such a conclusion and she explained. The Midwife told her to go to the hospital and be seen by a doctor.

My heart descended, as I dialled a doctor's number. To make the long story short, we finally learnt the baby died intrauterine at 25 weeks, a missed abortion. The doctor told us to go home and come back the next day for the baby to be expelled.

I have always thought that bonding between man and baby is not necessarily strong till after birth. However, I found myself in deep pain after the fact.

I have read (on *americanpregnancy.org*) *that the bond between a pregnant woman and the baby growing inside her is unique. A woman can begin bonding from the moment she has a positive pregnancy test. Bonding for the father may start as he experiences physical signs of the baby, such as seeing an ultrasound picture or feeling the baby kick. However, especially for men, real bonding may not develop until after the baby is born. This is why men may seem less affected by loss by miscarriage.*

I asked myself why I was hurting. I hadn't known this baby. Apart from the ultrasound, I had not known him, and beside the baby kicking, I did not have any serious contact with this baby. And yet I discovered that I loved him *like crazy.* I seem to remember that I wasn't hurt as much as I was angry. My heart was filled with anger and resentment. I didn't know who else to blame, but God. I thought that it was cruel of Him allowing such a thing to happen to me or especially, to my wife and baby. I remember receiving the news of the miscarriage, kneeling down on my knees, looking up to heaven and asking the Father, God, to heal this baby and bring it back to life. Yes, I dared asking God to breathe life back into the dead baby in my wife's womb. I felt I had the right to ask for such a thing from God seeing I was a Christian and I had never asked for much from Him.

At the same time, I had heard that there was a group of pastor evangelists who had been in the area for some days, conducting crusades and praying for the sick and performing all sorts of deliverances. That night I ran to find the place they were holding the crusade, desperate to save my baby. I came back home to get my wife, who I took with me in the cover of the night for prayers.

When we reached there, there were so many people such that it was very difficult to get through to the stage. But we finally made it, but the pastors were busy laying hands on people and praying for the sick; at the same time many were being invited to the front to testify of what the Lord had done for them. I thought that maybe, just maybe, one of those testimonies would come from me.

When we reached the front, amidst all the commotion, a pastor spotted us and he asked me what I needed God to do. I explained to him what we were told at the hospital, and that I wanted my baby to live. He laid hands on us and declared that the boy shall live.

The next morning we went back to the hospital believing that the ultrasound would show a heartbeat, this time. There was no heartbeat, still.

When they finally expelled the baby from my wife, I was not allowed to touch it owing to some African traditional belief that the man is not supposed to touch the dead foetus. I withdrew from everybody else and cried. I prayed to God for strength. I wondered why the same power that was at work within me could not save my baby. I am a Christian, and I had prayed for God to protect and keep my baby alive by the mighty power of the Holy Spirit. I always thought that things like this would not affect me to that point, but I was wrong.

Perhaps I will not be able to tell you why you are hurting, but I believe that the Lord could not have orchestrated such a misfortune. I have come to learn that certain things will happen to us as children of God, but not because God wants them to happen. Throughout that time, I learnt that I loved this baby way before it was born. I understood that the love I had for this baby was a miracle. I understand that there was something about a father's love that nobody has understood yet.

When Jesus was born, there was joy in heaven. We know this by the multitude of angels who sang praises to God in Luke 2:13-14. This is to indicate how much the Father had already loved the Son. I know how painful it is to lose a baby, the anger and disappointment. Disappointment in the things you have put your faith in. But in the long run, as a man, you are required to lead your family through this grieving process. Allow yourself to be filled by God. It does not help that everybody is expecting you to be strong and brave throughout this process, but the Holy Spirit is your only ally.

After all these things had passed, I found myself on my knees, again. I was praying to God and seeking answers. I didn't want to ask Him why any of those things happened. No, I just wanted to be with somebody who loved me, cared and was stronger, wiser than I. I had no other place to run to, but back to God. As I prayed, I heard strong calm come over me, as if a hand rested on my shoulders, and palming me on the back, a still, small voice said, "Don't worry, I am always with you. I have always been with you." I cannot express how much comfort that gave me.

Right now, a year later, we have been blessed with a bouncing baby boy. He is just what both my wife and I have always wanted. Glory be to God. Stay with God, and do not lose hope. He is right there with you.

Chapter 2

The Purpose for Work

Everything the LORD does has a purpose. It is difficult sometimes to understand why God does certain things, but He does it for the good of us. I remember a friend asking why God created the Anopheles mosquito (malaria mosquito) when He knows that this particular insect is responsible for the millions of deaths as a result of the malaria in Africa.

I will not go into the conversation we had about the malaria mosquito with my friend. No, I am merely showing you that there is always something which man thinks was created for no good. Like Lamech, we may think that we need comfort concerning work. We may think that God was merely punishing us because of the Sin. But God worked for a purpose and He commanded man to work for a purpose. There are only three purposes for work I want to show you in these pages, but I am sure there are more.

Number 1

To Bring or restore Order

The importance of work cannot be overstated. If the maker of heaven and earth and all life worked, then it is only prudent for the creation to follow in His footsteps. The bible shows us that from the beginning, the Father has been working on all fronts to advance His own purposes for the good of His people. But, as I always say, in order to understand the purpose for anything, it is better to go back to the place it was first mentioned in the bible. Here is where we see the word *work* first:

Genesis 2:2, *And on the seventh day God ended his work which he had made; and he rested on the seventh day from all his work which he had made.*

It is amazing to notice that God was working all six days. He was all alone in the universe, and yet He worked and only rested on the seventh day. How was it that even when there was nothing in the earth but disorder and chaos, the Father found something to work with? (Genesis 1:2)

Indeed, the LORD started His work by restoring order to the world.

Jeremiah 4:23-25, *I beheld the earth, and, lo, it was without form, and void; and the heavens, and they had no light. I beheld the mountains, and, lo, they trembled, and all the hills moved*

lightly. I beheld, and, lo, there was no man, and
all the birds of the heavens were fled.

A glimpse into the state of affairs in the earth is given by the prophet, Jeremiah. There was no form, the earth was empty; the heavens had no light. One would wonder where the birds of the earth had fled to. But there was no man. God had to restore order and bring tranquillity to the earth before placing the man.

The LORD planted a Garden and placed the man in there to manage it. But for all these things to have fallen into place, God had to work; He did not rest until He saw that all was good. God replaced the bad with the good and made sure that He had put a keeper to make sure things remained well.

Anything beautiful or good you have seen, somebody worked to put it in place. There is nothing proper or correct without having been put in place by work. We have seen tremendous works of art or architecture, amazing skill in sports or music; but all that has only been the result of the much work others have put in.

Correctness is order. No person wants to listen to poorly produced music or watch inadequately developed talent in sports because there is nothing good about them. They are terrible and horrible to the ears and the eyes. But perhaps that's the only thing this does. What about a poorly skilled surgeon? A fraud emergency physician? No person can afford any of these because they could mean the only thing standing between you and your untimely death.

This world has different categories of people whose work means life or death: doctors, nurses, pharmacists, and pilots, drivers and electricians, meteorologists, chefs, politicians and so on and so forth. These different units could mean the difference between life and death or between good and terrible food.

Imagine being served by a person who was not willing to put in the work on any level; you would suffer in the hands of someone you trusted. We see botched bodies everywhere and taste horrible food. We hear of airplane crushes everywhere, some of them genuine but some owing to human insufficiencies. It is true that most mistakes can be genuine, but when there is a blatant disregard for diligent work in everything people do, then that is negligence.

In the scriptures, we see God engaging in work not for the sake of it, but for to create and restore order, to restore beauty to the earth.

John 17:4, *I have glorified thee on the earth: I have finished the work which thou gavest me to do.*

Even Jesus calls what He did in the earth, work. He tells the Father that He had finished the work He was given to do. Salvation did not come easy. Jesus had to work for it, free as it may be.

Number 2

To fulfil God's purpose

Perhaps one of the most important purposes for work is this one, to fulfil the purpose of God. No person can live outside the purpose of God and still be normal. Man was created to live in the purpose of God and it is only in Him that the man finds fulfilment. The man who has neglected this principle has ended up regretting life and despising destiny.

John 9:4, I must work the works of him that sent me, while it is day: the night cometh, when no man can work.

Jesus had the Father's purpose driving Him. He walked with the Father and fulfilled His calling. Jesus said that the Father loved Him because He gave His life to die, only to take it back (John 10:17). Every person is expected to live their lives as though they lived for God; man was not designed to live outside the plan of God.

Every man in the Bible had a purpose. God called them for a specific task. Jesus' purpose was to bring and give life to dead man. He came so that whosoever believes in Him should not perish but have everlasting life (John 3:16). But He did not just become the life giver overnight, He put in a lot into His ministry; He had challenges but walked out victorious. One time He requested for that *cup of suffering* to be lifted from Him, and yet He remembered that what He had come to fulfil was not His own will but the Father's (Luke 22:42).

God said to Jeremiah, the prophet, *"For I know the thoughts that I think toward you, saith the LORD, thoughts of peace, and not of evil, to give you an expected end,"* Jeremiah 29:11.

The LORD was simply telling Jeremiah that the man was designed to live within the precincts of God's thoughts. The plans of God toward him were not harmful or dangerous, but they were of peace; they were plans to give him an expected future full of hope.

Men today are always told to let their children grow up and decide what they want on their own. But how will they know what is right if they are not raised in the right way? The whole idea of letting a child grow and decide what they want is absolutely unbiblical. Solomon advised against this when he admonished:

> **Proverbs 22:6,** *Train up a child in the way he should go: and when he is old, he will not depart from it.*

Leaving a child to the world and expecting him or her to learn the right way is cruel. Children are supposed to be taught the right way to go so that they don't depart from it when they grow old. This is important because every parent should realize that children are a gift from God. No person gets a child on merit; they are given to you by God as a love gift. But these children are also carriers of divine destiny. They carry the will and purpose of God in them.

A child is a human being who has his or her own individual calling in the plan of God. They are supposed to learn the ways which will help them realize that purpose and walk in the plan of God. Parents are to know how to raise these children in such a way as to allow them realize the purpose of God in their lives. But all this takes a lot of work. Parents should commit to working hard in making sure their children are not only equipped for divinity, but also for the world. It is really a sad thing to have a child and letting the world educate them.

This is not only so for children, but for spouses, as well. The Father instituted marriage for one purpose only, and that is, to enable both partners work together to achieve the plan of God in their individual lives. God knows that when his work is fulfilled in your life as an individual, then His work in you, as a couple, will also be completed. It is only when we have learnt to promote each other individually will we realize our collective potentials. Each person shall be held accountable for their role in building or breaking the other. People should learn that it is not by chance or mistake that they are with somebody, the Father has a beautiful plan for marriage and He desires that all men and women know this.

But no person ever only fell into their destiny without putting in a lot of work. Mary, the mother of Jesus did become the mother of the Lord, eventually, but she had to carry that child full term and delivered him in a manger; Esther had to work to become desirable to the king and she became queen; even the prophets had to suffer tribulation in their efforts to get the message of the LORD across. The man or woman of God should learn to work and achieve God's purpose in his or her life.

Nummber 3

To find fulfilment: to get a reward

Besides working to accomplish God's purpose, there is working to get a reward. That is to say, every person needs to be rewarded for the good work they do. The opposite may also be true, for instance, if any person's work is poor then their reward would be none.

Rewards come in many ways. Many people will tell you that having the results of the work they do would be a good reward for them, but some want to be appreciated in certain ways. I am sure I speak for many when I say that it doesn't matter what my work accomplishes, seeing the results is good, but being shown appreciation beats them all.

Every person wants to be appreciated; to be told that they have done a good job. We want to be noticed and crowned on some level. The apostle Paul, said, *"Henceforth there is laid up for me a crown of righteousness, which the Lord, the righteous judge, shall give me at that day: and not to me only, but unto all them also that love his appearing."1 Timothy 4:8.*

The Holy Spirit also says, *"Behold, I come quickly: hold that fast which thou hast, that no man take thy crown." Revelation 3:11.*

In whichever way you want to look at it, this means that there is a reward at the end of this earthly journey. God has set rewards for all those who will fight the good fight of faith. The LORD demands truth, diligence and righteousness. Do you see a man successful in the work of the ministry? He is truthful, and diligent. Thanks be to God for we function only in His righteousness.

But what about our earthly walk? Wouldn't it be good to receive rewards in the earth also? Indeed, this aspect is also just as important. Calvin Coolidge said this:

"No person was ever honoured for what they received. Honour has been the reward for what he gave."

I am inclined to agree with Mr. Coolidge. Honour is a beautiful thing. It is a good thing to be recognized and honoured for what you do. But all this comes to us only when we have given, first. The world today has different awards for almost everything. Today we have awards in Science and Technology, Military and patriotic honours, Humanities, and business and management. The fact is that there would not be space to mention all of the accolades there are in the world.

It is simple, really; the world knows that not only is it morally right, but it is also admirable to award a person deserving. But these awards and honours only come to men and women who have given themselves to working hard to change the way the world works for the good of the people. These works are selfless.

Jesus asked for a reward:

John 17:4-5, *I have glorified thee on the earth: I have finished the work which thou gavest me to do. And now, O Father, glorify thou me with thine own self with the glory which I had with thee before the world was.*

This was not a thing to ask lightly. Jesus saw His work and he knew that He had finished the work He was sent to do by the Father. He not only realized His own, but the Father's dreams, as well. But He still wanted a reward from His

Father. The Father granted His request and glorified him (Philippians 2:10).

Today, people are rewarded in different ways, but in a world where money means so much, financial rewards are always a good motivating factor. For example, people are encouraged to study hard and excel in their professional careers not only because of self-actualization, but because of the better paying employment opportunities that better education brings with it. So people work hard in their studies for different motivations, but they all strive for a reward at the end of the day.

Chapter 3

The blessing of Work

Ruth 2:12, *The LORD recompense thy work, and a full reward be given thee of the LORD God of Israel, under whose wings thou art come to trust.*

God created man to work. He knew that man could not just be created to live idle lives full of free things. He taught Adam to appreciate work and recognize that without it there cannot be any fulfilment. In the opening scripture, Boaz prayed a simple wish for Ruth; he prayed that God recompensed her and rewarded her fully for her work under whose wings she had trusted.

There are two things to consider, here, the worker and the rewarder. The person engaged in work should know who he works for. Paul said that he knew who he believed in and he was persuaded that the same would take care of what he had trusted him to do right to the end. (2 Timothy 1:12). In this particular passage, the worker knows that the employer was capable of rewarding him.

Today, we are plagued with corrupt leaders almost everywhere you look. Many people have thought for so long that the church was supposed to be a shining beacon, exposing to the world that corruption had no place in the plan of God. This has not been the case. Many people have found themselves victims of the clergy, taken advantage of because they were too trusting.

Leaders in many places do not know how to reward. They purport to be good leaders and yet they stand number one examples of oppressors. The apostle, Paul, said this about them:

2 Timothy 3:1-7, *This know also, that in the last days perilous times shall come. For men shall be lovers of their own selves, covetous, boasters, proud, blasphemers, disobedient to parents, unthankful, unholy, Without natural affection, trucebreakers, false accusers, incontinent, fierce, despisers of those that are good, Traitors, heady, highminded, lovers of pleasures more than lovers of God; Having a form of godliness, but denying the power thereof: from such turn away. For of this sort are they which creep into houses, and lead captive silly women laden with sins, led away with divers lusts, Ever learning, and never able to come to the knowledge of the truth.*

Such leaders are men full of themselves, lovers of themselves more than lovers of God. They covet, are boastful, proud and blasphemers; ungrateful, cruel, fierce and trucebreakers. These men have absolutely no regard for truces and contracts; they break every promise they make and are high-minded. These leaders are detestable to God.

The African continent is infamous for corrupt leaders, dictators and self-centred leaders. This is seen by the many examples portrayed by the many who have failed to give up power when the time came; many have clung to the power even when they were unwanted. The people of countries continue to suffer poverty and lack of proper health and sanitation when their leaders continue to misappropriate tax-payers' moneys and donor Dollars. This is unbiblical and is a slap in the faces of the voters.

However, corruption is not only in Africa or third world countries. No, it is spread world over, even in the so-called *developed, capitalist, industrial countries.* Corruption in these countries is so fecund that it is at a very grand scale. It may not have anything to do with donor moneys, but it could have much to do with international trade and stock exchange markets; and we may not have to mention international and domestic drugs and guns running.

I am not here to talk about corruption, as some understand it; I want to point the reader to the fact that it is these kinds of corrupt practices which cause genuine works look unprofitable. Men and women work very hard, giving themselves to selfless service, and yet the people who always seem to *make it* in life are the corrupt. There is a very unfair advantage corruption places over the men and women who are faithful and diligent in their dealings.

Because of this perceived unfairness, many people have gotten themselves in problems; it has caused many people to err from the faith and pierced themselves with many sorrows. Paul warned that this would be the result of focusing much of our love on money, (1 Timothy 6:10). Solomon said, "Envy thou not the oppressor, and choose none of his ways." (Proverbs 3:31). This is important because once a person who loves money and is self-centred, goes down that road, they will stop at nothing to get what they want. It may not necessarily be money; it could be a job, a girl or even property.

But God has a different plan for you. He has set for you a path you should walk. Do not indulge in corrupt practices only so you can get ahead in life. There are many who have ended up selling their souls to the devil through witchcraft, sorcery, Satanism etcetera, just for money. This has resulted in so many heart breaking calamities in their families and in their own personal lives. Tormented by the devil, they have realized too late that the deal was not worth making. The devil has taken their peace, their joy and love; placing unreasonable and unachievable demands on them such that they have lost their families and friends.

But the LORD says,

Deuteronomy 16:15, Seven days shalt thou keep a solemn feast unto the LORD thy God in the place which the LORD shall choose: because the LORD thy God shall bless thee in all thine increase, and in all the works of thine hands, therefore thou shalt surely rejoice.

The works of your hands are important to God. This means that God is interested in the work you put in. Everything you do matters to God. It doesn't matter whether you're studying or are in employment; whether you are an entrepreneur or an athlete, God wants to bless the works of your hands. You may not be working to get paid, for instance, but are only working to see results, God is still interested. Some of you have been trying to lose weight for a very long time and you haven't been able to hit that target- have you asked God to bless the works of your hands?

Work not only causes us to be blessed, it is a blessing on its own. Without work, man is idle and lazy, not amounting to anything. Do you think that man would have been able to accomplish the great discoveries of the past eras? Without work Orville and Wilbur would not have invented, built and flown the first successful airplane; Isaac Newton would not be known today. The world is full of men and women who have changed the way the world worked.

Instead of thinking about work as a curse, think of it as a blessing. It is the one blessing with the power to bless more. As long as you work hard, the LORD promises to bless that work of your hands. No person should work and not be blessed. The Bible says that the blessing of the LORD, it maketh rich, and he addeth no sorrow with it, (Proverbs 10:22).

Do you see any work which has turned into a burden, a sorrowful engagement? That is not from God. As long as there is God in it, the Christian will have no reason to be sorrowful because God's blessings are not accompanied by sorrow. Instead, the blessing of work should make you rich. The word of God guarantees that when you work, exercise this blessing of work, you will definitely become rich in every sense of the word.

Chapter 4

God is not lazy

If I was writing notes on this subject, the title of this chapter would suffice. Any person reading this knows that this is unfathomably true. All from Genesis to Revelation, we see the wonderful works of God in the earth and in our lives. The Father has been working from the outset, and He will still be working for eternity.

He completed His work of creation in six days and He rested on the seventh. But His work of salvation was only beginning; working in and through judges, kings, priests and prophets, He mapped out a clear path for the salvation of all mankind until it all worked out as planned (To understand more on this subject, please read my book called, *The Holy Spirit and You, Understand the Person*).

Before the LORD begun working on the earth, we see the Holy Spirit moving above the waters. The Spirit of God was not in heaven relaxing with the Father; He did not say to Himself, "I will wait till the Father speaks a word and then descend to the earth." No, He was in the earth hovering, searching for the spoken word to perform it. The Spirit of God did not stop moving until the word was spoken, and He jumped right into action.

Jeremiah 1:12, Then said the LORD unto me, Thou hast well seen: for I will hasten my word to perform it.

Even long after the LORD rested from His work, God is still working. Here, He tells us that He always watches His word to perform it. There are times the Word of God may happen in one's life, but sometimes, the LORD has to hasten it to perform it.

Hebrews 4:12, *For the word of God is quick, and powerful, and sharper than any twoedged sword, piercing even to the dividing asunder of soul and spirit, and of the joints and marrow, and is a discerner of the thoughts and intents of the heart.*

The word of God is also working. The word is quick (alive, living) and powerful, sharper than any two-edged sword. This is remarkable. The word of God is not dormant and idle. It is always working and piercing to the dividing asunder of soul and spirit, and of the joints and marrow. The word is a discerner of the thoughts and intents of the heart.

The man, was created to be like God. No person was created to be lazy. The Oxford Advanced Dictionary defines lazy, as being disinclined to work or exertion. This means that a lazy person is one who is unwilling to work because of mild dislike or disapproval. It does not necessarily mean this is the way a person is, it only means this person deliberately makes the conscious decision not to work; he is not incapacitated in any way, but rather, he has only decided to see his challenge and elected to be lazy.

The Holy Spirit warns us against laziness:

Proverbs 24:30-34, *I went by the field of the slothful, and by the vineyard of the man void of understanding; And, lo, it was all grown over with thorns, and nettles had covered the face thereof, and the stone wall thereof was broken down. Then I saw, and considered it well: I looked upon it, and received instruction. Yet a little sleep, a little slumber, a little folding of the hands to sleep: So shall thy poverty come as one that travelleth; and thy want as an armed man.*

The results of laziness are there for even the lazy to see. Poverty strikes like a visitor and lack, as a robber. If you neglect to study you will fail; if you don't till the ground, you will not eat; and if you choose to be mediocre in your execution of duties, you will always be considered last for promotion, you may even lose your employment.

Many Christians say they are Christians but don't want to put in the work to enhance their spiritual walk with God. They don't want to study the word, pray (and fast), read books and listen to spiritual sermons. Some won't even go to Church, bible study or fellowship. It is usually the same people who don't want to give for the advancement of the kingdom of God. You need to know what the bible requires of you so that you live according to God's purpose.

Luke 12:47, *And that servant, which knew his lord's will, and prepared not himself, neither did according to his will, shall be beaten with many stripes.*

The apostle Paul understood what God wanted him to do, but he also knew that he could not afford to be lazy about it. Even though the grace of God was upon him greatly, he laboured more than anybody else. The grace of God granted him supernatural relevance and his labour was noticeable by the church then, and today.

1 Corinthians 15:10, *But by the grace of God I am what I am: and his grace which was bestowed upon me was not in vain; but I laboured more abundantly than they all: yet not I, but the grace of God which was with me.*

Some Christians think that they can simply go to Church and let the anointing teach them; they abscond lectures and neglect to create time for studying. This is foolish as it will lead to you failing. You cannot afford to sit around, and expect to make it in the end. The LORD will bless the works of your hands, but if your hands are up to nothing, there will be nothing to bless.

But this situation is different from the one where somebody works really hard but he or she is not getting results. Remember, work was designed by God to produce results, good results. The person who works diligently and faithfully is guaranteed of success.

Chapter 5

When work doesn't pay

But what happens when that work is not paying off? What happens when there is a lot of exertion on all fronts and yet there is no yield? It means something is wrong.

The Bible tells us that we should study to show ourselves approved unto God, worthy workmen that need not to be ashamed (2 Timothy 2:15). Well, in this case, the person is studying but there seems to be shame. His study is not paying off.

There are a number of things to do in such cases.

1. **Study (Continue studying)**

   Sometimes we may try everything in our power to do something but nothing seems to pay out. This is frustrating because it defeats the purpose of work. The whole point of work is to see results and know that what you're doing is working. When what you do produces less to no results at all, it is time to re-evaluate your work. Sometimes we get less from work because we are not doing it right. Sometimes we just lack more information on how to do the job. More study and research helps. You need to commit to attaining more information.

The Bible says,

Proverbs 4:7, *Wisdom is the principal thing; therefore get wisdom: and with all thy getting get understanding.*

There is never a time any person had enough knowledge. There is not a place in this world that has everything, not even the internet. I have found myself looking for certain knowledge on the internet and came out with nothing. Make it a principle in your life to always look for knowledge and understanding. If you're in formal employment, it is advisable to set yourself up for trainings and workshops. Advancing your studies further is always a good way to go. Education has an almost miraculous way of placing people way ahead of others.

2. *Ask for help*

It is always a good thing to ask for help. Sometimes you may not know everything and you may not necessarily have the time to learn some things. It is wise to ask for help from somebody who already knows what you need, this is cheaper and faster. There is always a help meet for everyone. In some situations, it is not good for you to be alone, and it is your responsibility to know which help is suitable for you. The LORD said it was not good for the man to be alone in the work he was assigned by God, and so He made him a suitable help. He could have let Adam do everything alone, but He knew that most of the time, it is not good for any peerson to be alone.

Deuteronomy 32:30, How should one chase a thousand, and two put ten thousand to flight, except their Rock had sold them, and the LORD had shut them up?

Ecclesiastes 4:9, Two are better than one; because they have a good reward for their labour.

Two people who bring the same thing to the table may not go as far as two who bring different, but relevant skills together. The two should complement each other in order to achieve the common goal. Sports are a good example of how team players bring their different sporting attributes to make a formidable team.

Cesar Chavez said, *"You are never strong enough that you don't need help."*

Any person striving for success should know this truth. Do you want to reach the skies? It only takes the strong, and like Rona Barrett said, *"The strong individual is the one who asks for help when he needs it."*

Your role is to recognize that you need help.

Kings of Old understood this principle and depended on treaties and allies. Today, countries still use this principle. They know that in order to realize efficient trade or social equality, treaties and deals are essential in achieving a common goal.

3. **Pray**

As much as this sounds simple, it isn't. Prayer takes patience and commitment. There are somethings which need you to pray and ask God for solutions. You have done everything humanly possible and yet nothing seems to work; it is time you looked for the supernatural. Sometimes, like in the case of Daniel, the answer might be held up in the heavens by an evil spirit (Daniel 10:12-13).

Paul also told the Church to pray:

2 Thessalonians 3:1-2, *Finally, brethren, pray for us, that the word of the Lord may have free course, and be glorified, even as it is with you: And that we may be delivered from unreasonable and wicked men: for all men have not faith.* This was important because for the gospel to have had free course, there should have been a lot of prayer involved. After all the natural efforts to advance the gospel had been done; the people had given money and other resources, the apostles had been given accommodation, and were standing in front of the people to speak, there was always need for the supernatural to advance the word of God in the hearts of men.

There are evil spirits in this world which will stop at nothing to see you suffer. Some people are so wicked that they will bewitch you on account of your own success. The bible does say that no witchcraft will bring you down (Numbers 23:23). The Christian may be facing supernatural opposition in their life. This can only be moved by prayer. It is in prayer that God gives you divine strategies to defeat the enemy and conquer the obstacles of progress. Some things need you to pray and fast, for this may be God's instruction to you. However, speaking in tongues may do a lot more than ordinary prayer. Christians are admonished to speak in tongues whenever they pray for this is the miracle that moves mountains. (For more on tongues, please read my book, *Tongues of What? Know your language*).

Don't be lazy in prayer. Be very specific and speak to the LORD in all honesty. Always look out for the LORD's voice. Be very attentive in prayer and study the word of God diligently because it is in there that God will reveal Himself to you.

Prophet Bernard said that the safest place to be, is in the spirit, because no one can find you there. Always pray and walk in the spirit, the same way that you live in the spirit (Galatians 5:25).

4. *Be patient*

After you have done all these things and you are sure that everything is legal with man and God, be patient.

When God had done everything and accomplished our salvation in Christ Jesus, He did not fast track His plan to forcing all of man-kind to be Christians. No, He was patient:

2 Peter 3:9, The Lord is not slack concerning his promise, as some men count slackness; but is longsuffering to us-ward, not willing that any should perish, but that all should come to repentance.

God knows that without patience, all the work that he had done would not count for anything because many would perish. But God does not want anyone to perish, but that all should come to repentance. The Father believes in the work He did in Christ Jesus and He has faith that it is working.

When you have faith in God and believe that what you have done is in his purpose, you will be patient to see what results it will produce.

Your work will surely pay off, believe in God and His promise to you, He will perfect it. If you choose to be inpatient, you may only undo the work God is doing in your life. There can really be no shortcut to achieving your dreams.

Conclusion

In conclusion, we now understand that work has always been in the plan of God. There is no fulfilment without God.

God Himself worked hard in order to bring order and tranquillity. Work is the blessing that keeps giving and does not come with sorrow.

Indeed, there will always be challenges; any work of God is always opposed by negativity. Sometimes, these are natural in order to strengthen the individual, but with God nothing shall be impossible. The Father promises that nothing shall come to you which is beyond what you can bear.

If God be for you, who or what can be against you? Nothing. God will cause you to prosper in your work. The best you could do is enjoy what you do and honour God and love others.

Do not be self-centred and always learn new things. Beyond this, there is no limit to how much you will excel in life. The LORD bless you.

About the Author

Andrew Simwanza is a Zambian pastor.

He is founder andpresident of the Chrisma Life Church, currently headquartered in Zambia. He is also the author of the Kingdom Insight Devotional series. He is passionate about the gospel and desires to see every Christian walking in the light of God's word.

Andrew believes that men and women are changed by words. He writes because he believes this is the surest way to secure knowledge for the present and the future generations.